Constructing Big Air

by Jillian Sullivan

CAMBRIDGE
UNIVERSITY PRESS

Chapter 1

The snow shines on the Big Air jump. It looks just like a snow jump in the mountains. Only yesterday it was steel scaffolding in a dirt yard. Now, nine metres up on the tower, my friend Heath bends to strap into his snowboard.

Will the jump I've made be high enough? Is it safe? Will Heath get up the speed he needs to clear the fourteen metres **gap** in the air before he hits the landing?

I go and stand far back in the **VIP** area to watch. It has the best view of the gap. I want to see how the jump flows. Will the jump be too poppy and make Heath go too high? Or will it be too flat, and he'll crash into the **massive** gap? Heath is my craziest friend. He's the one willing to be the **guinea pig** and try out the jump for everyone's safety.

The event crew and the other riders stand looking up at Heath. He drops in and straight lines it. The jump gives him enough height for a stylish **540**. He clears the gap, but only just.

Time to get the salt out. I take a bag of salt up the steps to the take-off point of the jump and throw handfuls of salt onto the snow. It will harden the snow and let the riders go faster and higher. Then I give the all-clear and the riders grab their boards.

Chapter 2

It all started three months earlier when I got an email from the event manager for the Queenstown Winter Festival. They had the funding and the go ahead for the Big Air competition to be held for the first time in the town instead of up on the ski field. If I wanted it, the job of building the jump was mine. I leapt at the chance.

I loved competing in the Big Air competition, but an injury now means I build jumps instead. I try to design jumps I would like to use. I try to design jumps that give thrills to both the riders and the **spectators**.

The first thing I do when I've been given a job is check out the **site**. The site they've chosen is an empty lot just outside town. There's an old garage on the lot with a clear space in front of it. Then the lot drops down to another level.

I pace out the size of the lot and get a good feel for it. After some quick **calculating**, I decide that this will work just fine. I can build the jump up and over the garage. The hill in front of the garage provides a natural dirt landing.

I take digital photos of the site. Then I do drawings with measurements on them. I'll need this information when I sit down to design the jump.

The most important thing I have to decide is the design of the **drop-in ramp**. How high will I make it? Five metres? Eight metres? And what will the angle be? How long should the flat bottom be before going up the **take-off ramp**?

For it to be perfect, the drop-in ramp needs to provide enough speed for the snowboarders to clear the gap. The higher they can go and the bigger the gap, the more chance they have to go hard and **nail** their jumps.

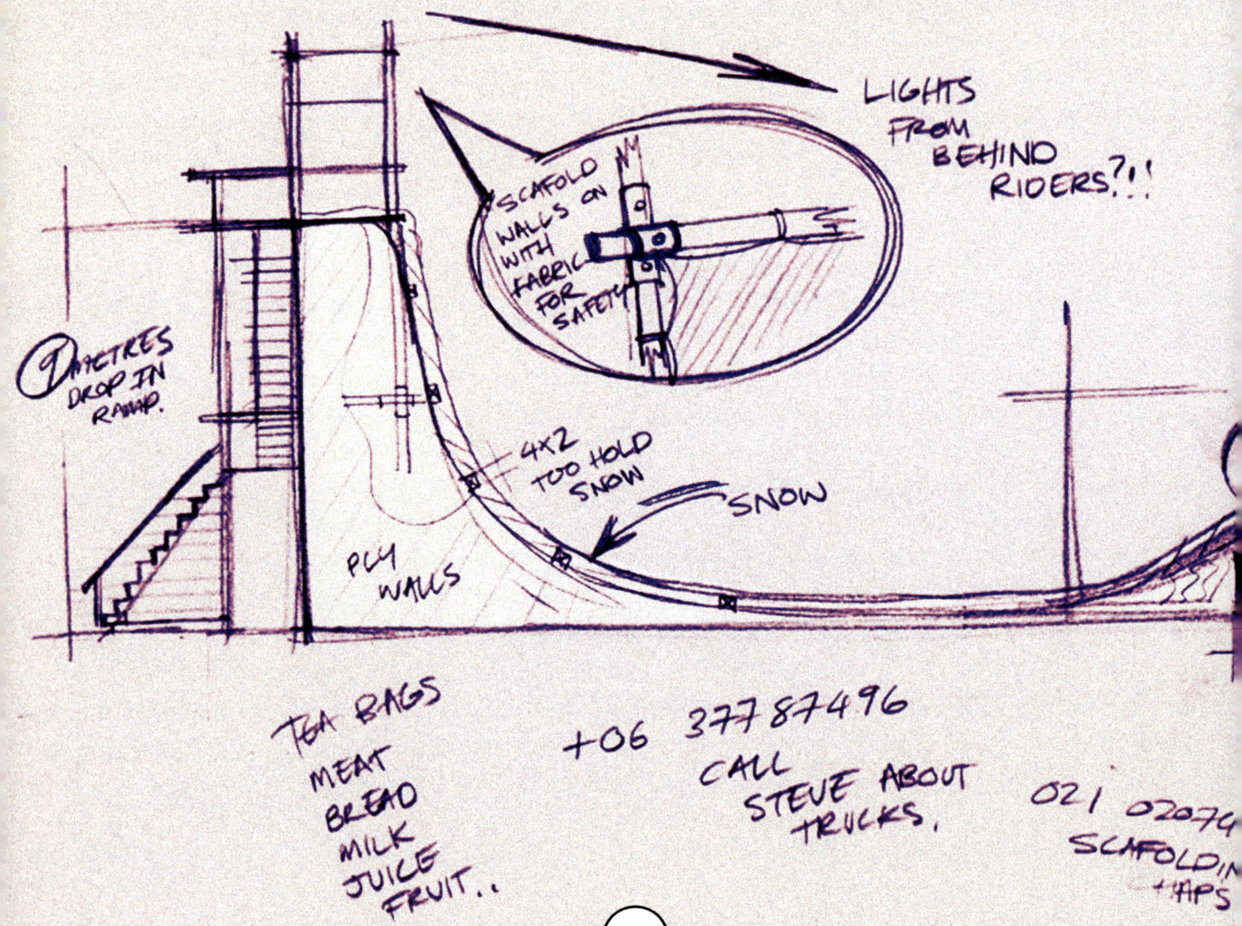

The last jump I designed had a seven-metre-high drop-in ramp. I decide to make this one nine metres high. By making the ramp this high, I can make the gap bigger.

The gap will be fourteen metres. The snowboarders will be jumping over a gap as wide as a house. The riders will need to be going at least twenty kilometres per hour to get over the gap. I think my nine-metre-high ramp will give them that speed. I sure hope so!

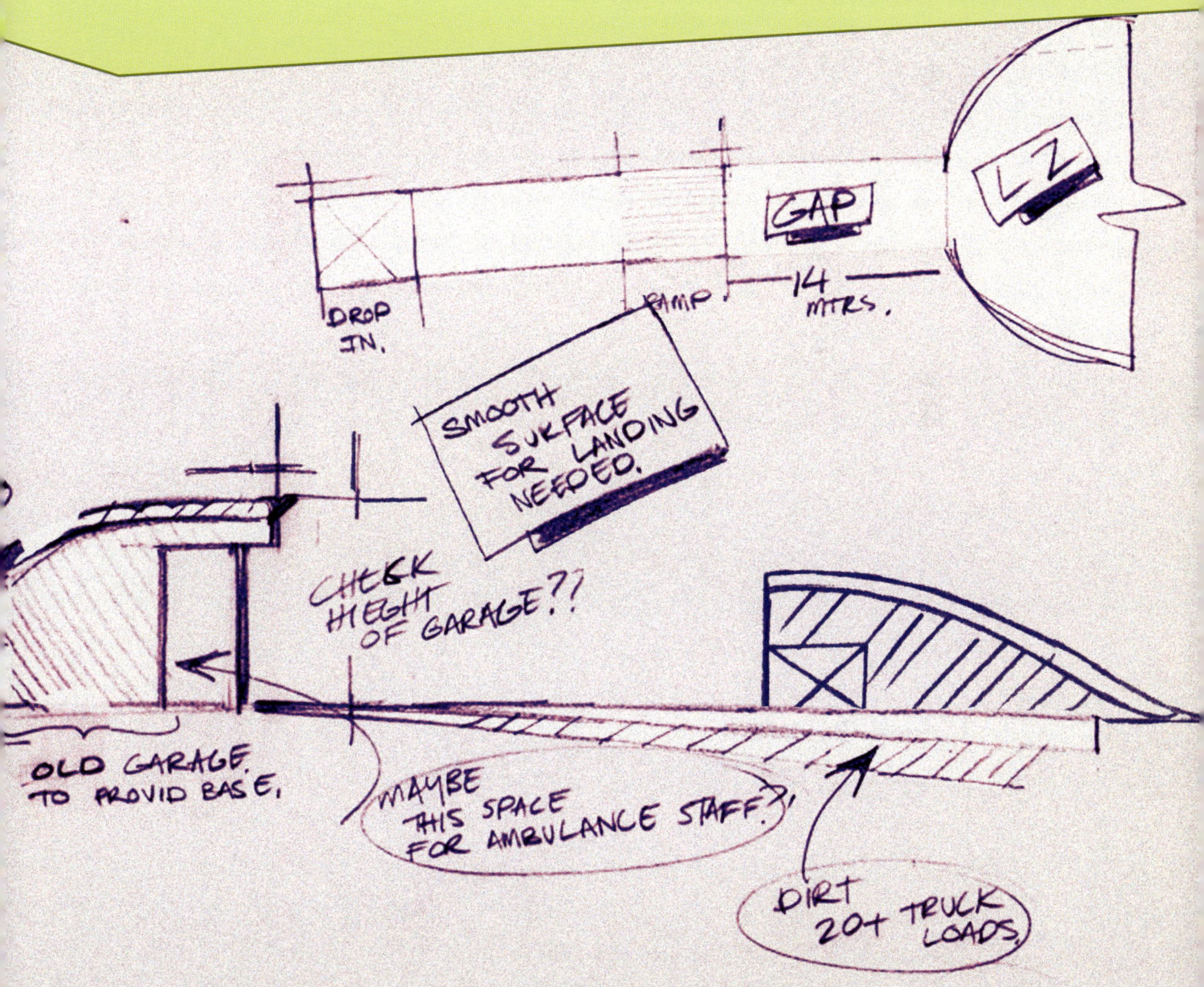

Chapter 3

I pick a **scaffold** company to do the work. We meet at the site so that I can show them what I want done. We mark where everything will go with spray paint. They start building the tower two weeks before the event.

The hill on the site is too steep to be a natural landing for the jump. To be safe, the **run-out area** needs to be smooth. Twenty truckloads of soil will do the trick. After they deliver the soil, a bulldozer spreads it out. Now I'm happy with the landing. It should be safe for the snowboarders.

The scaffolders finish building the jump the day before the competition. Now it is a big structure with a staircase going up to the launch platform. The surface is covered in plywood. We attach boards to the side of the ramp to hold the snow in. Then we nail 4x2 planks on the plywood. These boards will keep the snow from sliding down the ramp.

Snow was the one thing I couldn't do without. I contacted a local ski resort and talked them into sponsoring the event by providing truckloads of snow. On the morning of the competition, fifteen truckloads of snow arrive. Half the snow is dumped at the landing and run-out area. The other half is dumped in a big pile next to the jump. Now I need my workers with their shovels.

I hired local snowboarders to help me shovel snow onto the jump and to maintain the jump on the night of the competition. Some of these snowboarders will be competing and they want to work on the jump to make sure it is a good one.

We shovel the snow into big flat buckets that we carry up the steps to the top of the jump. Then we pack the snow in, starting at the top and working our way to the bottom. It takes five of us five hours to get the snow on the jump and smooth it down.

Chapter 4

By two o'clock the jump is ready. I look up at the sky. Rain could be my biggest enemy now. It would turn the snow to slush or ice and make it dangerous to jump. The sky is clear. Thank goodness!

I turn and give the thumbs up sign to Heath. The other riders and event crew watch as he takes off. When he nails that first big 540 jump, clears the gap and stomps his landing, I feel the relief go through me.

The rest of the riders rush to the tower to get as many practice jumps in as possible. I put a worker at the bottom of the steps so only four people at a time can go up to the top. It can get dangerous with too many people up at that height. There's also a worker at the top. He will radio the riders' names to the judges and the **emcee**.

By five o'clock the lights are installed and on. I've placed lights all the way down the tower so that it looks like daylight on the drop-in ramp. Spotlights shine on the gap so the riders don't feel like they are launching out over blackness. Lights shine on the landing area, too. Each light is placed so it won't shine in the snowboarders' eyes.

Just as the sun starts setting, the **spectators** begin to arrive. The judges are set up and ready in their tent. The DJ has the music **amped** up. The competition is about to begin.

I start to relax. What I want to do now is have fun watching the riders pull off their awesome tricks. I keep a constant eye on my jump. Is the take-off point still hard? Is the landing okay and not too rutted? I place workers on the sides to maintain the snow.

Heath's extra practice pays off. He nails a **720** in front of thousands of people. He comes third in the competition.

As for me, my three months of hard work has paid off as well. The jump looks awesome lit up in the night sky and its height allows the snowboarders to show off their skills. The competition couldn't have gone any better. I feel great.

Glossary

amped	amplified or playing loudly (slang)
calculate	to work out using maths
drop-in ramp	the steep ramp you descend from at the top of a ski jump
emcee	the master of ceremonies or host of a show
540	a ski jump in which you spin sideways one and a half times
gap	the space between the take-off ramp and the landing area
guinea pig	someone willing to try something new
massive	very large
nail	to perform a trick perfectly (slang)
run-out area	the place where a snowboarder comes to a stop after landing a jump
scaffold	a supporting structure made out of steel
720	a ski jump in which you spin sideways twice
site	place where something happens
spectator	a person who watches a sport or event
take-off ramp	the upward curving part of the ramp at the bottom of a ski jump
VIP	very important person